Cat Spelled Backwards
Doesn't Spell God

Portraits of Divine Dogs

By Jeff Selis

CHRONICLE BOOKS

SAN FRANCISCO

Copyright © 2000 Jeff Selis

Printed in Hong Kong.
Set in Trade Gothic and Meta Plus Book.
Concept Design: E. Hawthorne Hunt.
Typographic Design: Wendy Reynolds, Olive Design.

First published 1998 by Wieden & Kennedy, Inc.

Library of Congress Cataloging-in-Publication Data available.
ISBN: 0-8118-2817-4

Distributed in Canada by
Raincoast Books
9050 Shaughnessy Street
Vancouver, BC V6P 6E5

10 9 8 7 6 5 4 3 2

Chronicle Books LLC
85 Second Street
San Francisco, CA 94105

www.chroniclebooks.com

The first reason this book exists is because of a generous grant from Wieden & Kennedy, Inc.—an advertising agency in Portland, Oregon. I was awarded the grant after entering my idea in Wieden & Kennedy's first Slime Mold Award contest. This award was designed to encourage employees to realize their creative potential in any medium. My idea was to publish a book on dogs—a book that would convey the uniqueness and importance of dogs. I never imagined it would actually win.

The book immediately became a top seller, and within three weeks I had sold all 3,000 copies. You'd have thought I'd died and gone to heaven. And just when I thought it couldn't get any better, it did. Chronicle Books saw the book and made an offer to pick it up and republish it! Unbelievable. Aside from a couple of tweaks from the original, what you now hold in your hands is what started as a little nugget of an idea inside the head of a guy who just happened to work at the right place at the right time.

I hope you enjoy the book. I had the time of my life making it. As I said in the original, I cherished every drop of drool on my clothes, every lick on my cheek, and every nose print on my lens.

Many thanks to Wieden & Kennedy for throwing me such a huge bone. And many thanks to Chronicle Books for throwing me another!

—Jeff Selis

This book is dedicated to my mom and her dog, Max.

Thank you, Mom, for getting me over my fear of dogs by bringing home our first dog, Whiz. And thank you for always going back on your word after saying, "Never another dog!" In my life, I'll never be without one.

I'll miss you forever, Mom. May you and Max rest in peace.

I love you.

Your son, Jeff

Buddha

Buddha *loves* his belly rubs.

He also has a deep affection for watermelon, corn chips, and raisins. If he finds himself getting a little too soft in the middle, he will head out to do some serious trail running or take to the mountain for some cross-country skiing.

Buddha is two years old and has yet to find the humor in the noise that his owner makes through the empty paper towel tube.

Little Bit

Little Bit enjoys nothing more than hanging out on her master's lap.

She is a purebred dachshund who hates being called a wiener dog.

Gus

The thing Gus hates the most is being hosed down, but that doesn't keep him from doing what he loves to do most—roll around in the neighbor's compost pile. P-U!

Gus was named after Augustus McCrae of *Lonesome Dove* fame. And like Augustus, he *does* have a way with the ladies.

El Toro De Las Nubes

You can call him Tor.

Being the runt of the litter has never stopped Tor from being a social butterfly. He loves company, and he'll lend an ear to anything except country music.

On a walk he loves to stop and smell the roses. Really.

Katie

Katie loves to spin around on her hind legs for Crunchy Corn Bran cereal and to get her nails painted every trip to the beauty parlor.

But she'll sit in her "pouting chair" whenever she is left behind.

Katie is five years old and can't stand carrots.

Charlie

What floats Charlie's boat is when his mom comes home from her job and takes him on a long run.

He's not your stereotypical Doberman—the one thing Charlie can't live without is his binky. That's right, his binky.

Still, one would be wise to think twice before testing him.

Jack

Jack takes flight almost as often as United Airlines. He also loves to fetch and fancies cat poop if the litter box isn't cleaned.

Although he's a very lovable pup, Jack has a running feud with German shepherds. They seem to like to pick on dogs with lots of spots.

Cy

Cy was named after the legendary pitcher Cy Young. While he never could have hit a Cy Young fastball, he definitely could have gone to bat with him in a cookie-eating contest. Cy loves a good cookie.

He is ten years old and very proud and protective of his brand-new baby sister.

Alexander and Joshua

Alexander and Joshua love kids. Lucky for these two, their home is full of them. They love it when the kids take them on long walks through the neighborhood. When the kids aren't around, they are happy to just lie in the shade.

Alexander has six toes on one of his back paws.

Brenainn (pronounced bray-nin)

Brenainn is an Irish wolfhound who was born in Dublin and immigrated to the United States as a wee pup. Though his accent isn't as thick as it used to be, Brenainn upholds his Irish tradition by marching in the St. Patrick's Day Parade every March. It is by far his favorite day of the year.

Brenainn opposes war, fleas, and pills.

Romeo

Forget Juliet, the only thing this Romeo would die for is a fresh-baked cookie.

Romeo is a Great Dane puppy who is still learning as he goes. For instance, whenever he sees another dog on television, Romeo will walk behind the TV set in search of this four-legged stranger.

Romeo's parents live in fear of the day he discovers the Internet.

Riley

The life of Riley must consist of a daily dose of fruits and vegetables. He loves his fruits and veggies. If only kids could be more like Riley!

Riley also likes to ride in the car, unless of course it's a trip to the groomer. Other than the vacuum cleaner, there's nothing he despises more than being bathed and brushed.

Otis

Everyone calls him a pit bull, but Otis is really a purebred Staffordshire bull terrier who's probably the friendliest dog you will ever meet. The only thing lethal about him is his tongue. Given the opportunity, he might just lick you to death.

Otis loves any kind of movement, whether it's pacing around the living room furniture with his favorite toy, or taking a long hike on the weekend.

The only thing Otis hates is when his parents have to go to work.

Bart

Hide the varmints, because Bart is a full-on terrier and he loves a good chase. One time Bart's parents brought him to a Thanksgiving dinner, but no one told him that the host's pet rat, Rocket, wasn't on the menu.

Oops.

Ellie

Ellie is a product of the Greyhound Placement Association. Having spent her early years at the track, Ellie retired and found a cozy home in the city. An unfortunate accident at the age of seven cost Ellie a leg, but she never lost her spirit. Ellie now spends much of her time visiting nursing homes.

For kicks, she likes to hang out at the playground, where she'll take on anyone in the hundred-yard dash.

Ellie is now nine years old—sixty-three for you and me.

Hoover

Hoover marks his territory in the big city. However, city life comes second for this dog, who relishes every chance he gets to go chukar hunting with his mom and dad in the wide-open country.

Hoover was named after the vacuum cleaner for the speed with which he sucks down his food.

His favorite thing to clean is the family cat, Selma.

Kramer

Kramer is the lovable protector of a family of four. His favorite thing to do is stand guard at his mom's big bay window overlooking their street.

Kramer is such a good protector that he once thwarted a robbery attempt on his mom in the parking lot of the area grocery store. He then cornered the bad guy until someone with two legs came and took him away.

This dog deserves a medal.

Phoebe Snow

Phoebe Snow has been white-water rafting and survived a swim down a class-4 rapid. Want more? She will sing for beer.

While normally outgoing and warmhearted, Phoebe Snow is easily annoyed by people with high-pitched voices who try to pick her up.

Lucy

According to Lucy's owner, she is the best dog that has ever lived. Her owner also adds that when people climb into his truck they say "P-U!," but he doesn't smell anything.

Lucy loves doing tricks for treats, especially cheese.

Her pet peeve is going potty on wet grass.

Choco

Choco is a friendly guard dog who protects his family's home twenty-four seven. Prowlers beware. He may not see you coming, but he will definitely smell you. And you don't want that.

By the way, Choco has his fair share of first-place show ribbons. It's a hobby when he's off duty.

Shawnee

Shawnee loves people, kitties, and back rubs.

She takes a walk with her mom every single night.

Spunky as ever, she's eighty-three going on thirteen.

Norman

A stray, Norman was window-shopping for a home when he found a bargain
he couldn't refuse.

Norman is now in charge of security at his adoptive mother's antique shop.
He greets paying customers with a smile and a wag of the tail.

Friedrick

Friedrick is a weimaraner who loves to climb rocks and trees. Weimaraners have large feet with which they can clutch things.

Friedrick's favorite thing to clutch is his momma. She's the one who provides him shelter, feeds him treats, and takes him on those "oh so aromatic" walks in the park.

Bogey

Bogey's four favorite words are *chicken-basted rawhide bone*. He will clean his teeth on one for hours. Say the word "bath," however, and this dog will hightail it the other way.

Bogey was found at the Humane Society in Las Vegas. His owners spotted him there and decided to take the gamble. Eight years later, he's proved to be a pretty safe bet.

Double Bogey

Anna

Anna is the pride and joy of her doting owner. She goes everywhere her master goes—whether it's to work, to the beach, to the store, or to bed.

She's showered with praise, attention, and gifts; every lady should be so lucky.

Brandy

Brandy is following in some pretty impressive footsteps. The two poodles before him, Jocho and Beau, lived to the ripe old ages of fifteen and fourteen, respectively.

Brandy's unique coloring made for a difficult choice of a name. The alternate was Cognac. Either way, he's definitely a dog worth toasting.

Here's to your health, Brandy.

Caesar

Perhaps more suited as a groundhog, Caesar is transfixed by his shadow on a cloudless day. Legend has it that one day he stared at his shadow from sunup to sundown. Spring couldn't come soon enough for this pup.

When questioned about his feelings on dalmations, Caesar had no comment.

Lucy D

Lucy D gets wiped out playing games with her big brother and big sister in the big yard of their big house.

Rest and relaxation are her big rewards until it's time to go again.

Baby

A trip to the nearest park is a pretty sweet deal, but there's nothing Baby loves more than eating hot dogs and watching TV.

Baby is three years old and can channel surf with the best of them.

Spot

Spot's favorite pastime is chasing her tail. The only sight crazier than Spot chasing her tail is her reaction to the recycling truck when it pulls up on Monday mornings. She absolutely loses it!

Spot is a product of the Bull Terrier Rescue League and is now a happy and almost sane nine years old.

Chuck

If you look up "dog paddle" in the dictionary, you might just see a picture of Chuck. All his favorite activities revolve around water. He loves sailing, fishing, and just plain swimming. Heck, he's ecstatic if he gets sprayed down with the garden hose—so a day at the beach is like winning the lottery.

Chuck loves all people, animals, and insects. His master says he wouldn't even hurt a flea. Crazy dog!

Barkley

With enough hugs and kisses for the entire world, Barkley's overflowing affection
still wasn't enough to keep his first owner from abandoning him in an orchard.

Barkley was rescued, however, and promised a home for good.

He continues to love everyone—except the vet.

Basia

Basia loves her mommas the most. She also loves back scratches and long naps. Then again, who doesn't?

Basia is seven years old and has yet to learn to walk on linoleum floors.

Micho (pronounced MEE-ko)

Micho is a white German shepherd who gets her daily exercise fetching balls, rocks, and sticks in the back of her parents' two-acre home. In fact, she will retrieve anything you throw her—except grapes.

Micho is three years old and loves to snack on "kitty roca."

Titan

He may be the neighborhood bulldog, but he's no neighborhood
bully. Titan is the most popular dog on his block.

The only thing he loves more than your attention is vanilla ice
cream. It's his reward for being good.

If only we could all have such incentive.

Rocky

Quite the knockout, Rocky lives for his daily workout, whether it's a good run or a simple walk around the block.

Rocky is in his second year and loves to "KO" spiders with his long, pink tongue.

Sydney

Sydney is a puppy who loves anything that's not hooked to the ground. This includes her momma's new Nikes, dirty underwear, and sweaty socks.

Sydney also loves to pick strawberries and raspberries off the vine.

At her young age, the only thing she doesn't like is reading the daily newspaper. She poops on it instead.

Callie

Callie loves her human sister Jenny who suffers from epilepsy. She gives her the love she needs every single day.

Callie is especially excited about the family's new lake house—a place to rest and relax and fetch the balls thrown into the lake by Jenny.

You're a good dog, Callie.

Paddy

Paddy's favorite treat is a cherry tomato. She actually has her own tomato plant in the garden that she harvests on her own every summer.

Paddy wakes at the crack of dawn each morning so she can get an early start chasing squirrels. She has yet to catch one, but Paddy is determined to succeed before her dog days are over.

Binky

Binky loves Bongo.

Bongo

Bongo loves Binky.

Kersey, Porter, and Buck

Kersey, Porter, and Buck are the true definition of Neighborhood Watch. The only time they let down their guard is during the annual block party—they just can't claim responsibility for those funny-looking humans dancing in the middle of the street.

Kersey, Porter, and Buck were named after three favorite Portland Trail Blazers. Too bad they don't have a brother named Jordan.

Giani

Giani's mom keeps a bamboo fountain in the sunroom of their home. When Mom's not around, Giani loves to duck her head under the water and remove the rocks, one by one. Then she hides them around the house. When the rocks are gone, she takes a seat in the fountain as if it were her own personal spa. Then Mom replaces the rocks, and the process starts all over again.

Giani was named after a comet discovered by Carl Sagan.

Sherlock

Sherlock is a black-and-tan coonhound mix who has many of the same attributes as the master detective himself. Whether tracking a raccoon, an opossum, or a bone buried long ago, he is always searching to solve a mystery.

Sherlock is ten years old and digs up new clues daily.

Boo Radley

Boo Radley likes everyone and everything, which is amazing since he was abandoned twice before the age of six months. If you give him some food you've got a friend for life. His expression at the dinner table says, "Are you going to eat that?"

Boo Radley is now four years old and will never bite the hand that feeds him.

Chelsea

Chelsea was born in New York, where she lived with a family that was busting out at the seams. Something had to give. Chelsea was the odd one out. Fate took over and Chelsea waved good-bye to her family and the asphalt jungle and made her way to the lush and green Great Northwest.

Chelsea now enjoys car rides in the country, long walks in the park, and just kicking back to the mellow sounds of old Dean Martin.

Seems Chelsea never had it so good.

Geronimo

Call him Joe for short but, please, don't call him short. Joe has a serious little man's complex.

Joe got his full name after perching himself on his mom's window ledge five stories above a busy downtown street. Had Joe not been coerced back in with a tasty treat, no one knows just how far he would have gone to prove his doghood.

King

King, formally known as CH. TLC's King of Hearts V Breaker, is a prized show dog who loves to travel and strut his stuff.

He can't stand the heat, but he loves to be in the kitchen, especially when there are fresh-baked goodies around.

King is four years old and weighs a mere 205 pounds.

Big Daddy

If Big Daddy were to run an ad in the doggie personals it would read:

*Charming, self-absorbed, sexy male seeks companion who loves
giving affection and snacking on pigs' ears. Should cherish walks
in the park and have lots of patience for a marker's mentality.
Sucker for Italian greyhounds.*

You go, Big Daddy.

Molson

Molson is golden. He is the resident dog at a hospice facility for people with life-threatening illnesses.

Molson will go from one room to the next spending quality time with any patient who wants or needs it. Molson has quite a bit of insight into what patients are going through. He had cancer himself; even had chemotherapy and lost his hair for a while.

He must be an angel.

Barley

Only about two inches off the ground when standing on all fours, Barley becomes "Air Barley" when his mom takes him to the park to throw around the Frisbee. After a game of fetch he likes to cool his belly in the nearest mud puddle.

Barley is two years old and can't stand having his nails clipped.

"Vedorrie!"

When Vedorrie's not relaxing around her stately home, she's probably out traveling the globe. She's been to Brazil, France, Italy, and Holland.

Her favorite airline is KLM, because the flight attendants get a kick out of speaking her name. In Dutch, Vedorrie means "Damn it!"

Vedorrie's favorite meal is waffles.

Woody and Rosie

Woody and Rosie love to hang out at the park, but be careful if you're having a picnic nearby because these two won't hesitate to invite themselves over for a bite—of food that is.

These littermates are "love sponges" constantly seeking attention. Their love runs so deep they even share a queen-sized bed with their humans.

Timmie, Sophie, Lucy, Charlie, Frazier, Otis & Maggie May

These siblings were all taken in and nursed back to health by one amazing woman. Otis, Frazier, and Timmie were all abandoned. Charlie lost his master to AIDS. One way or another, they were all in need of some serious TLC.

All are thriving now in their mother's pet shop. There, they await the day a permanent owner will come and take them home, but if the right person doesn't come along, they've got a pretty sweet deal just where they are.

Oscar

Oscar is a Humane Society rescue. He will drool over
anything good that comes his way, whether it's his
nightly walk with his worshiped master or a table
scrap from his big brother Matt.

Oscar is a lucky seven years old.

Bleu

Bleu's favorite thing to do is watch people eat—he figures if he stares long enough he's going to win out. He's right.

The only thing Bleu won't eat is parsley. Go figure.

Bleu misses his brother Max very much. What he misses most is licking the goobers away from Max's eyes first thing in the morning.

Max

Max was spoiled rotten. He loved nothing more than sleeping in the middle of the twelve down pillows that decorated his mom's queen-sized bed. Max also loved Bleu, who took up the rest of the bed with his long body and legs. Mom loved her dogs so much that she was content to sleep on the couch.

Max is now in dog heaven—a place where there are sure to be lots of pillows.

My Special Thanks Page

Special thanks to Hawthorne Hunt. Thank you, Hawthorne, for taking on the role of art director, designer, editor, etc. Other than making me put

a picture of your silly cat in this book, everything you did was perfect. You deserve a raise!

Special thanks to the Slime Mold Award judges (whoever you were) and Dan Wieden. I hope I done you proud.

Special thanks to Bill Davenport, Mike Yonker, Bedonna Smith, Paige Powell, Clint Ackerman, Michele Lefore, Lauren Ranke, Micaela Heekin, and Sara Schneider for your time, help, and support.

Special thanks to all those I called for advice and wisdom in the publishing world. Every cold call I made got a warm reception. Thank you.

Special thanks to the other Jeffs— Kling and Williams. Thanks for the title and the input. And also special thanks to Janet Champ for giving my dog such an eloquent voice on the back cover.

Special thanks to everyone I asked for an opinion.

Special thanks to all of the dog owners for your patience and excitement. Please buy lots of books for your friends and relatives.

Special thanks to my family: Momma, Duddy, Ronnie, Heather, Chet, Sam, Laura, Henry, and Sally. Thanks for indulging me. Really.

And special thanks to my ever-so-patient, loving, and beautiful wife, Alice. I love you. And Sam Cole, too!

Oh yeah, a special thanks to all the dogs, the ones I photographed and the ones I didn't. You're all worthy, and in my book, you're all gods.

Amen.